Life as a Private

on the

Lewis and Clark Expedition

by Jessica Gunderson

Illustrated by Colleen Madden

PICTURE WINDOW BOOKS

a capstone imprint

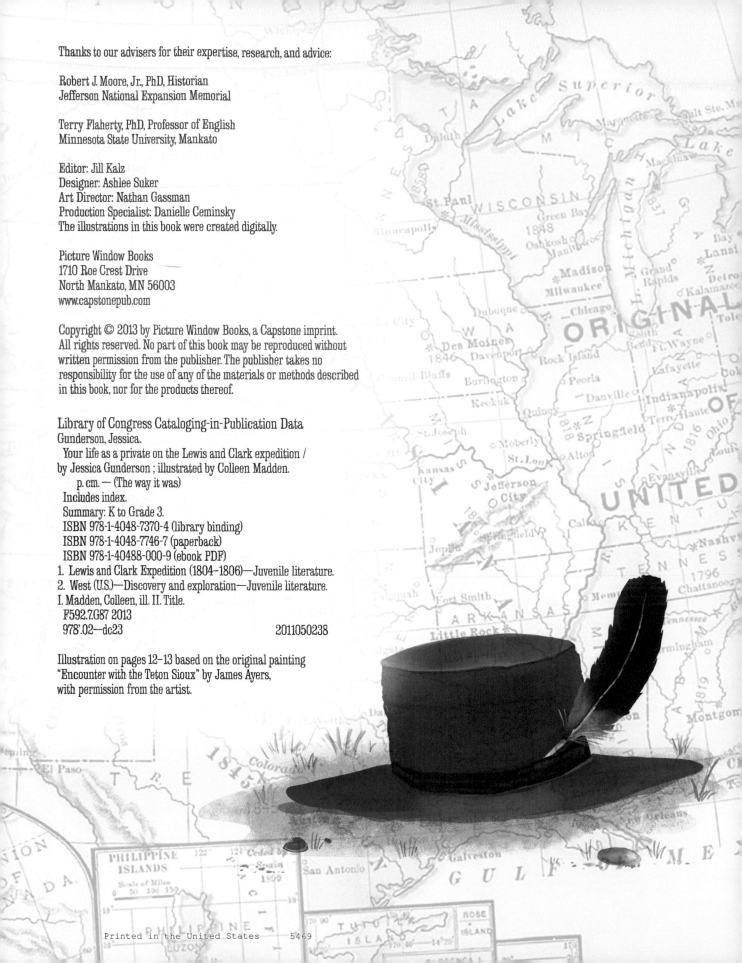

Thanks to our advisers for their expertise, research, and advice:

Robert J. Moore, Jr., PhD, Historian
Jefferson National Expansion Memorial

Terry Flaherty, PhD, Professor of English
Minnesota State University, Mankato

Editor: Jill Kalz
Designer: Ashlee Suker
Art Director: Nathan Gassman
Production Specialist: Danielle Ceminsky
The illustrations in this book were created digitally.

Picture Window Books
1710 Roe Crest Drive
North Mankato, MN 56003
www.capstonepub.com

Copyright © 2013 by Picture Window Books, a Capstone imprint.
All rights reserved. No part of this book may be reproduced without
written permission from the publisher. The publisher takes no
responsibility for the use of any of the materials or methods described
in this book, nor for the products thereof.

Library of Congress Cataloging-in-Publication Data
Gunderson, Jessica.
  Your life as a private on the Lewis and Clark expedition /
by Jessica Gunderson ; illustrated by Colleen Madden.
      p. cm. — (The way it was)
  Includes index.
  Summary: K to Grade 3.
  ISBN 978-1-4048-7370-4 (library binding)
  ISBN 978-1-4048-7746-7 (paperback)
  ISBN 978-1-40488-000-9 (ebook PDF)
1. Lewis and Clark Expedition (1804–1806)—Juvenile literature.
2. West (U.S.)—Discovery and exploration—Juvenile literature.
I. Madden, Colleen, ill. II. Title.
  F592.7.G87 2013
  978'.02—dc23   2011050238

Illustration on pages 12–13 based on the original painting
"Encounter with the Teton Sioux" by James Ayers,
with permission from the artist.

Your Role

Congratulations! You'll be playing the role of Private George Shannon in our play "Life on the Lewis and Clark Expedition." It's May 14, 1804. You're a 17-year-old young man from Kentucky. You and about 30 other volunteers are joining Captains Meriwether Lewis and William Clark on a trip up the Missouri River. Your goal? To find a route to the Pacific Ocean, following the rivers as closely as possible.

Mosquitoes? Frostbite? Creatures that lurk in the shadows? It's all part of the journey.

Let's go!

On a Mission for the President

Crowds gather along the river to say good-bye to your group. Some men on board are nervous, but you're not scared. You're ready for adventure. Your friends call you the best shot in Kentucky. As long as your gun's within reach, you'll be OK.

"Ready, men?" Captain Clark calls. You push off into the water, head upstream, and leave the St. Louis area behind.

OREGON

COUNTRY

LOUISIAN

PURCHAS

UNIT

SPANISH

N

W

E

S

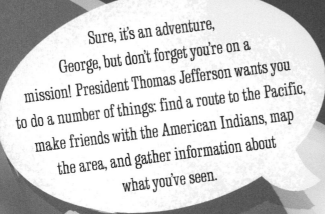

Sure, it's an adventure, George, but don't forget you're on a mission! President Thomas Jefferson wants you to do a number of things: find a route to the Pacific, make friends with the American Indians, map the area, and gather information about what you've seen.

"Go *that* way."

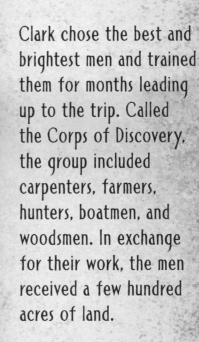

Clark chose the best and brightest men and trained them for months leading up to the trip. Called the Corps of Discovery, the group included carpenters, farmers, hunters, boatmen, and woodsmen. In exchange for their work, the men received a few hundred acres of land.

E D   S T A T E S

Backbreaking Work

SCRAPE! No one wants to hear that sound. The boat is hitting sandbars. You'll have to get out and pull. In no time you're sweaty. Your back aches. Clouds of mosquitoes and gnats stab your skin and buzz in your ears. **"This is no adventure,"** you grumble. **"Just hard work."** At this rate, it could be years before you reach the Pacific—if you reach it at all.

The goal was to travel about 10 miles (16 kilometers) per day. Most days, however, the group averaged about 4 miles (6.4 km).

ROBINSON CRUSOE

DOCTOR CLEM'S ELIXIR

Harder than you thought it would be? Well, don't even think about deserting. Another member of the expedition hated the hard work and flying pests too. He tried to run away but was caught and punished with a whipping. Ouch!

The expedition included a 55-foot-long (17-meter-long) boat, two smaller boats, and two horses. It also included 2 tons (1.8 metric tons) of supplies, including compasses, books, bullets, medicine, and gifts for trade.

What's for Lunch?

Time to eat. You help pull the boats ashore, and Captain Lewis blows a horn. It's a signal for the two men who went out hunting at dawn. They arrive with a deer and some rabbits. The cooks make a stew of the animals, with fresh wild berries for dessert.

After lunch you all pack up and head back out on the river for a few more hours. You can't wait to set up camp and get some well-deserved sleep tonight. **"Private Shannon!"** Captain Clark says sharply. **"You're on guard duty tonight."** So much for sleep.

The men ate whatever they could find, including berries, squirrels, buffalo, and fish. They also carried a limited supply of "portable soup," a beef paste that could be cooked. Corn, beans, and squash could often be bought from American Indians along the way.

The largest meal of the day was eaten at noon. Supper was more like a late-evening snack and consisted of leftovers from lunch.

On Guard

While the other men sleep, you and another private, John, stand guard. The night is quiet and still.

A twig snaps. Then another. You and John glance worriedly at each other. You raise your rifles. The rustling gets louder. Whatever it is, it's coming straight toward you!

The beast crashes into camp ... and plops at your feet, panting. It's Seaman, Captain Lewis' dog. You sigh and lower your rifle.

George Shannon was the youngest member of the Corps of Discovery. He once got lost in the woods for more than two weeks. He had no bullets and no food except berries and a rabbit he killed with a stick.

Meeting the Neighbors

In August you reach the plains. So far the American Indians you've met have been friendly. Captains Lewis and Clark have given them gifts of beads, mirrors, fishhooks, needles, and blankets.

But now you meet the Teton Sioux. The captains give them gifts, but they hold the boat and won't let go. They know you have more on board, and they want it. You tighten your grip on your rifle. Everyone's uneasy. Finally Chief Black Buffalo allows your group to pass.

THOMAS JEFFERSON PRESIDENT OF THE U.S. A.D. 1801

Lewis and Clark gave American Indian leaders a medal with a picture of President Jefferson on it. The medal was a sign of peace.

Wondering why your interpreter is waving his arms? No, it's not a game of charades. He's talking with the American Indians by using a mix of signs and words.

Winter at Fort Mandan

Brrr! It's freezing, and it's only October. Luckily you've reached the Mandan and Hidatsa villages. **"At last we can rest,"** you say. Captain Lewis laughs and says, **"First we have to build a fort."**

You chop wood and help build several cabins. Your fingers blister with frostbite. You've never been so miserable. You'd almost rather be bitten by mosquitoes than by frost. It will take two months to finish Fort Mandan. Two long, cold months.

Clark brought his slave, York, on the expedition. York hunted, fished, and cooked, just like the other men. He was even allowed to vote on where to camp near the Pacific. The American Indians, who had never seen a black man before, were amazed by him.

FORT MANDAN

New Members

One November day a fur trapper named Toussaint Charbonneau arrives. He wants to join the expedition. He has a Shoshone wife named Sacagawea and a child on the way. **"A woman and child might show the Indians that we come in peace,"** Captain Clark says. **"Plus,"** Captain Lewis adds, **"she can help us trade with the Shoshone for horses."** They agree to let the couple join them.

Born in February 1805, Sacagawea's baby, Jean-Baptiste, was well loved by the group. Clark took a special liking to him and nicknamed him "Pomp." Pomp grew up to be a mountain man, explorer, and guide.

Two Paths

By April the river has thawed. Several men return to the St. Louis area with maps and animal and plant specimens. The rest of you continue upriver in six canoes.

Soon there's a fork in the river. Which way? The northern branch is muddy, but the southern branch is clear. **"We're heading to the mountains,"** Captain Clark says. **"Water flowing from the mountains would be clear, not muddy."** Captain Lewis nods. He takes you and a few others to check out the southern branch. If you reach the waterfalls the Mandan told you about, you'll know you've chosen correctly.

Lewis and Clark were equals in command, but they had different personalities. Lewis was quiet and often walked onshore. He liked to write in his journal. Clark was outgoing. He spent most of his time on the boats with the men.

Don't look around for a map, George. You're one of the first explorers to ever travel beyond Fort Mandan. You'll have to trust the directions from Mandan chief Big White.

A Mighty Roar

WHOOSH! It's the roar of waterfalls. You're on the right path! But how will you get around them? **"We'll just pack up the canoes and supplies and carry them on land,"** Captain Lewis answers. Sounds easy, but it's not. After the others join you, it takes nearly a month to carry everything around the falls.

GREAT FALLS

"We should've packed lighter," you grumble. Captain Lewis glares at you. Then his face changes. He's looking at something over your shoulder. You turn. Grizzly bear! You aim your rifle and fire.

Whoa! You've seen many creatures on this journey, George, but none quite as scary as that *grizzly bear*. Before the Lewis and Clark expedition, grizzlies were unknown to people from the eastern United States. So were pronghorn antelope, prairie dogs, and mountain sheep.

21

Family Reunion

The Rocky Mountains loom ahead. And the wide Missouri River is now just a trickle. You can stand with a foot on each side! **"We'll need horses to cross the mountains,"** Captain Lewis says. You're glad Sacagawea is along. She can speak to the Shoshone. Plus, it turns out that the Shoshone chief, Cameahwait, is her long-lost brother!

The Hidatsa kidnapped Sacagawea from her Shoshone family at a young age. She was only 15 or 16 when she married the fur trapper Toussaint Charbonneau and joined the Lewis and Clark expedition. She wasn't a guide. But she did help the group find food and trade for horses.

Mountain Crossing

A Shoshone guide, Toby, leads the expedition into the mountains. Icy rain pours on your head, and wind whips your coat. As you climb the steep slopes, the horses slip and slide.

Food is in short supply. There's nothing around to shoot, not even a rabbit. **"I'm so hungry I could eat a horse,"** you joke. But Lewis looks at you, thinking. **"Let's butcher one of the horses,"** he suggests. Gross! But at this point, it's the only thing that can keep you all alive.

Before crossing the Rockies, the expedition hid their canoes by sinking them. They would pull them out again on the return journey.

Think eating horse is gross? Try dog! Dog meat was a common food among some American Indians. The Corps of Discovery ate nearly 200 dogs on the journey. Captain Lewis liked dog meat, but Captain Clark would not eat it.

Wild Ride

At last your tired bunch is over the mountains. The Nez Perce take you in, feed you, and help you build canoes. You set off on the Clearwater River. Now you're going with the current instead of against it. The boats fly downstream toward the Columbia River. You reach some fast-moving water, and the canoes jerk and lurch. **"This is fun!"** you say. **"Unless we all go under,"** John mutters. He's right. No one in your boat knows how to swim.

Only one man died during the expedition. Sergeant Charles Floyd fell ill only a few months into the trip. He died near present-day Sioux City, Iowa. Many historians think he died of a burst appendix.

Welcome to the Pacific

The Columbia River widens and slows. You smell salt in the air. **"Ocean in view!"** Captain Clark exclaims. Whew! You've made it! Although you haven't found a water route, you've blazed a path from the Missouri River to the Pacific Ocean.

But wait. It's not over yet. You have to build a winter camp. And then you still have to go back in the spring. You groan and settle in for a long, rainy winter.

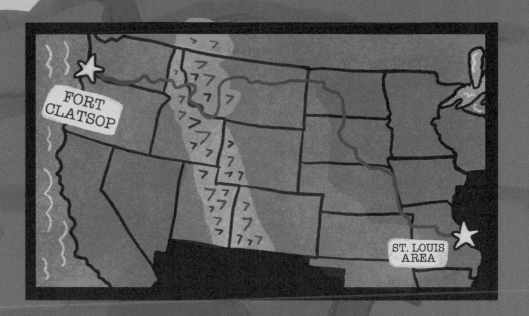

The Corps of Discovery stayed at Fort Clatsop, their winter fort, until spring. Of the 106 days at Fort Clatsop, only 12 were not rainy. Fleas and all kinds of illnesses were huge problems for the men.

Don't worry, George. The return trip will be much easier. You'll be going downriver most of the way. In the end, you will have traveled more than 8,000 miles (12,875 km) in two years and four months!

29

Finale

Take a bow, Private! You've traveled through uncharted wilderness to the Pacific Ocean. You met American Indians from many nations and saw creatures you didn't know existed.

Uh-oh. Are you itching? You don't have fleas, do you?

Glossary

appendix—a small, closed tube attached to the large intestine

desert—to leave military service without permission

expedition—a journey with a goal, such as exploring or searching for something

interpreter—a person who can tell others what is said in another language

mission—a planned job or task

private—a soldier of the lowest rank

route—the road or course followed to get somewhere

sandbar—a long island of sand in a river or along a coast

specimen—a sample that a scientist studies closely

volunteer—a person who offers to do a job, usually without pay

Index

More Books to Read

Ganeri, Anita. *On Expedition with Lewis and Clark*. Crabtree Connections. New York: Crabtree Pub., 2011.

Smalley, Carol Parenzan. *Lewis and Clark*. What's So Great about— ? Hockessin, Del.: Mitchell Lane Publishers, 2009.

Sutcliffe, Jane. *Sacagawea*. History Maker Biographies. Minneapolis: Lerner, 2009.

Internet Sites

FactHound offers a safe, fun way to find Internet sites related to this book. All of the sites on FactHound have been researched by our staff.

Here's all you do:

Visit *www.facthound.com*

Type in this code: 9781404873704

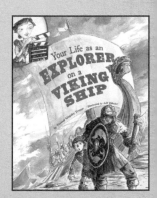

Super-cool stuff!

Check out projects, games and lots more at
www.capstonekids.com

Look for all the books in the series:

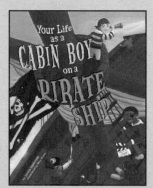

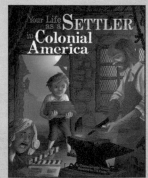